Super Simple Things to Do with Balloons

Fun and Easy Science for Kids

Kelly Doudna

Consulting Editor, Diane Craig, M.A./Reading Specialist

A Division of ABDO

ABDO
Publishing Company

To Adult Helpers

Learning about science is fun and simple to do. There are just a few things to remember to keep kids safe. Some activities in this book recommend adult supervision. Some use sharp objects or matches. Be sure to review the activities before starting, and be ready to assist your budding scientist when necessary.

Key Symbols

In this book you will see some symbols. Here is what they mean.

 Hot. Get help! You will be working with something hot.

 Adult Help. Get help! You will need help from an adult.

 Safety Glasses. Put on your safety glasses!

 Sharp Object. Be careful! You will be working with a sharp object.

visit us at www.abdopublishing.com

Published by ABDO Publishing Company, a division of ABDO, P.O. Box 398166, Minneapolis, Minnesota 55439. Copyright © 2011 by Abdo Consulting Group, Inc. International copyrights reserved in all countries. No part of this book may be reproduced in any form without written permission from the publisher. Super SandCastle™ is a trademark and logo of ABDO Publishing Company.

Printed in the United States of America, North Mankato, Minnesota
102010
012011

 PRINTED ON RECYCLED PAPER

Editor: Liz Salzmann
Content Developer: Nancy Tuminelly
Cover and Interior Design and Production: Oona Gaarder-Juntti, Mighty Media, Inc.
Photo Credits: Kelly Doudna, Shutterstock

Library of Congress Cataloging-in-Publication Data

Doudna, Kelly, 1963-
  Super simple things to do with balloons : fun and easy science for kids / Kelly Doudna.
    p. cm. -- (Super simple science)
  ISBN 978-1-61714-672-5
  1. Balloons--Experiments--Juvenile literature. 2. Science--Experiments--Juvenile literature. I. Title.
  TL610.D68 2011
  530.078--dc22
                            2010020825

Super SandCastle™ books are created by a team of professional educators, reading specialists, and content developers around five essential components—phonemic awareness, phonics, vocabulary, text comprehension, and fluency—to assist young readers as they develop reading skills and strategies and increase their general knowledge. All books are written, reviewed, and leveled for guided reading, early reading intervention, and Accelerated Reader® programs for use in shared, guided, and independent reading and writing activities to support a balanced approach to literacy instruction.

Contents

Super Simple Science

Want to be a scientist? You can do it. It's super simple! Science is in things all around your house. Science is in a candle and in a penny. Science is in aluminum foil and in duct tape. Science is even in water and in wool. Science is everywhere. Try the **activities** in this book. You will find science right at home!

Balloons

Learning about science using balloons is super simple! It takes science to burst a balloon. It takes science to make noise with a balloon. It even takes science to make a balloon fly around when you let go of it. In this book, you will see how balloons can help you learn about science.

4

Work Like a Scientist

Scientists have a special way of working. It is a series of steps called the Scientific Method. Follow the steps to work like a scientist.

1. Look at something. Watch it. What do you see? What does it do?

2. Think of a question about the thing you are watching. What is it like? Why is it like that? How did it get that way?

3. Try to answer your question.

4. Do a test to find out if you are right. Write down what happened.

5. Think about it. Were you right?

Keep Track

Want to be just like a scientist? Scientists keep notes about everything they do. So, get a notebook. When you do an experiment, write down what happens in each step. It's super simple!

 # Materials

string

penny

balloons

straight drinking
straws

ruler

flat head nails

pencil

hex nut

clear tape

wooden cooking skewer

birthday candle

measuring cups

aluminum foil

coffee mug

matches

yardstick

book

safety glasses

scissors

duct tape

baking dish

wool sweater

chairs

corrugated cardboard

That's Repulsive!

Can you keep two balloons from touching each other?

What You'll Need
- yardstick
- string
- scissors
- 2 balloons
- clear tape
- wool sweater, jacket, or coat
- stepladder (optional)

Static electricity pushes the balloons apart.

1. Cut two pieces of string about 30 inches (76 cm) long.

2. Tape one end of each string to the top of a door frame. They should be about 1 inch (2.5 cm) apart.

3. Blow up two balloons and tie them closed. Tie a piece of string to each balloon. The balloons should hang at the same level.

4. Rub each balloon on the wool sweater.

5. Let the balloons go. What happens? What happens if you move the balloons toward each other?

6. Put your hand between the balloons. Now what happens?

What's Going On?

Rubbing the balloons on wool gives them **static electricity**. This makes them move away from each other. When you put your hand between the balloons, they move toward it. That's because your hand doesn't have static electricity.

9

Let's Go Nuts!

How can you use a balloon
to drive everyone nuts?

What You'll Need
- safety glasses
- 2 balloons
- hex nut
- penny

The nut makes noise
inside the balloon.

1. Put on your safety glasses. Your balloon will **probably** burst at some point.

2. Put a hex nut in a balloon. Blow up the balloon almost all the way. Tie it closed.

3. **Grab** the top of the balloon with your whole hand. **Swirl** the balloon.

4. Keep swirling until the hex nut circles inside of the balloon. Use your fingertips to hold the bottom of the balloon.

5. What do you see? What do you hear?

6. **Repeat** steps 2 through 4. But this time use a penny instead of a hex nut. Now what do you hear?

What's Going On?

A hex nut has corners. When you swirl the balloon, the corners rub against the balloon. That makes a loud sound. A penny is round and smooth. It doesn't make as much noise.

11

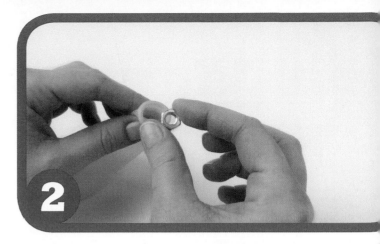

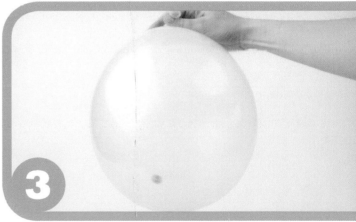

A Moving Experience

Can you move a mug using only a balloon?

What You'll Need
- coffee mug
- balloon

The balloon gets wedged into the mug.

The mug is lifted up.

12

1. Blow up the balloon part way. It should be a little bigger than the opening of the mug. Do not tie it closed.

2. Hold the balloon closed. Place it on the mug.

3. Blow up the balloon some more. Now tie it closed.

4. Lift up the balloon. What happens?

What's Going On?

A balloon's surface is rubbery. Adding air with the balloon on the mug **wedges** the balloon in. The rubbery surface of the balloon sticks to the mug. It's like it's holding onto the mug!

13

Jet Balloon

Why does a balloon fly like a rocket?

Air is forced out of the balloon.

The balloon shoots along the string.

1. Put the chairs 10 feet (3 m) apart. Tie one end of the string to one chair.

2. Thread the string through the straw. Tie the other end of the string to the other chair. Make sure the string is tight.

3. Blow up a balloon but don't tie it. Hold the end closed while you do the next step.

4. Move the straw to one end of the string. Tape the balloon to the straw. The opening should point to the closest chair.

5. Let go of the balloon. What happens?

6. **Repeat** steps 3 through 5. Blow the balloon up more or less than the first time. Or use a larger or smaller balloon. What happens this time? Why do you think that is?

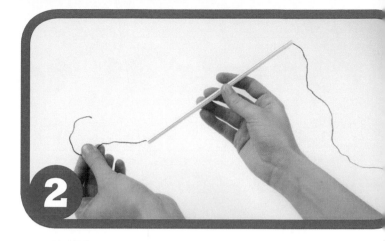

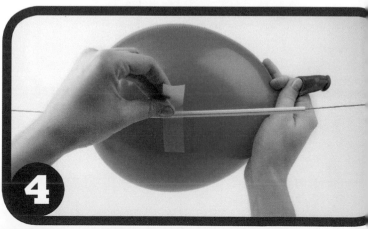

What's Going On?

When you blow up a balloon, it **stretches**. When you let go, the balloon quickly returns to its original size. All the air gets forced out of the opening. This makes the balloon shoot in the direction opposite of the opening.

15

Stick It to It!

If you poke a balloon with a sharp stick, it will pop, right?

The tape keeps the hole from getting too big.

The skewer doesn't pop the balloon.

16

1. Put on your safety glasses.

2. Blow up a balloon. Tie it closed.

3. Put a piece of tape on the balloon.

4. Gently push the sharp end of the skewer into the balloon through the tape.

5. Keep pushing the skewer into the balloon. What happens?

What's Going On?

Without the tape, the edges of the hole would pull away from the skewer. That would make the hole bigger and the balloon would pop. The tape keeps the hole the same size as the skewer. The skewer keeps the air in and the balloon doesn't pop.

Way Cool Water Balloon

Is a candle too hot to handle?

What You'll Need
- safety glasses
- 2 balloons
- small piece of aluminum foil
- birthday candle
- matches or lighter
- measuring cup
- water
- baking dish

Water keeps the balloon cool.

18

Part 1

1 Put on your safety glasses. Blow up one balloon. Tie it closed.

2 Press the foil around the bottom of the candle so it stands up. Have your adult helper light the candle.

3 Hold the balloon over the flame. What happens?

Part 2

4 Put about ½ cup (118 ml) of water in the other balloon. Blow up the balloon and tie it closed.

5 Put the candle in the baking dish. Hold the balloon over it. What happens this time?

What's Going On?

A balloon with just air pops right away when it touches the flame. That's because all the heat is in one spot. If the balloon has water inside, it doesn't pop right away. The water spreads the heat over a larger area. The balloon stays cool.

19

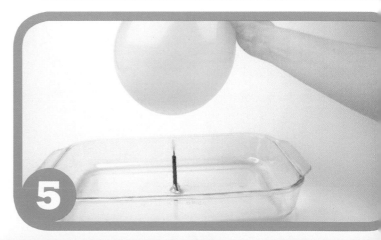

Bed of Nails

How many nails make the balloon fail?

What You'll Need
- 2 pieces of corrugated cardboard, at least 6 x 6 inches (15 x 15 cm)
- ruler
- pencil
- 101 flat head nails
- duct tape
- several balloons
- safety glasses
- a hardcover book

The book makes the pressure even.

No single spot on the balloon gets poked very hard.

20

Part 1: Make the bed of nails

1 Use the ruler to draw a **grid** on one piece of cardboard. The grid should have 10 lines in each direction. The lines should be ½ inch (1.3 cm) apart.

2 Have an adult helper do this step. Poke the nails through the cardboard where the grid lines meet. There should be 10 rows of 10 nails.

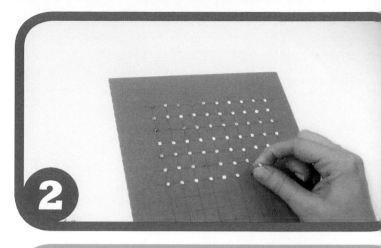

3 Carefully set the cardboard down. Put strips of tape over the nail heads. This will hold them in place.

4 Tape the second piece of cardboard on top of the nail heads. Turn the whole thing over so that the nails point up. This is the bed of nails.

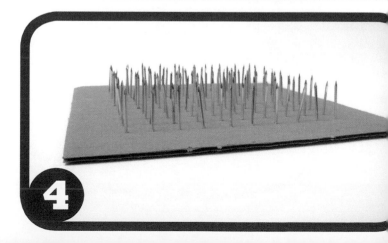

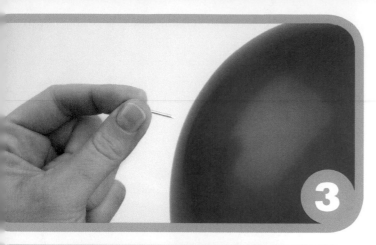

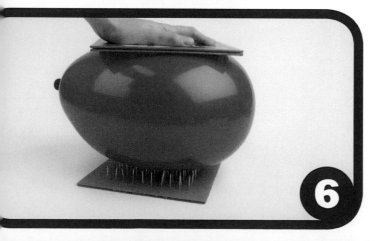

Part 2: Test the balloons

① Put on your safety glasses.

② Blow up one balloon and tie it closed.

③ Take the extra nail. Poke the balloon with it. What happens?

④ Blow up another balloon and tie it closed.

⑤ Carefully lay it on the bed of nails. Does anything happen?

⑥ Put the book on top of the balloon. Press down gently. What happens?

⑦ Keep pressing on the balloon. What happens?

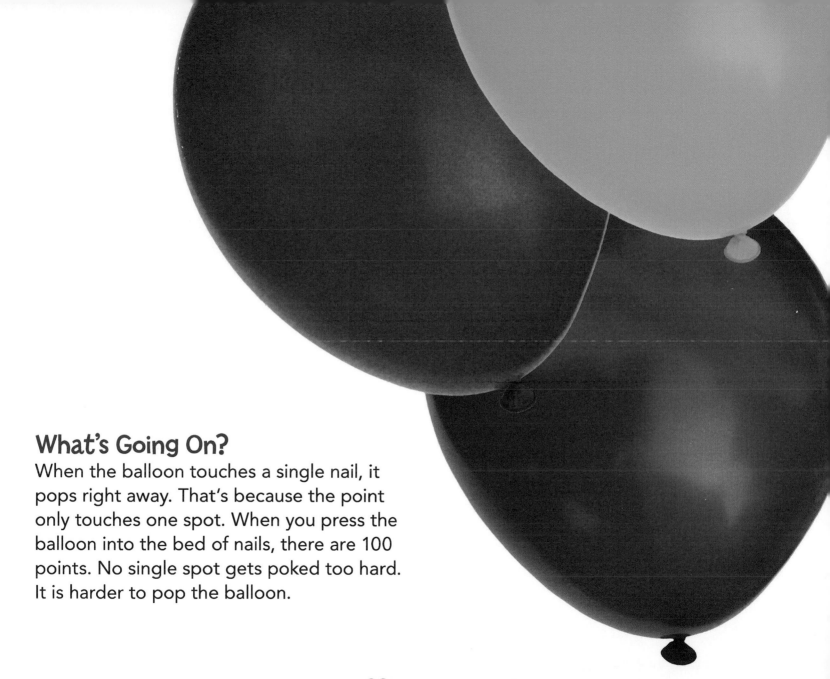

What's Going On?

When the balloon touches a single nail, it pops right away. That's because the point only touches one spot. When you press the balloon into the bed of nails, there are 100 points. No single spot gets poked too hard. It is harder to pop the balloon.

Conclusion

Congratulations! You found out that science can be super simple! And, you did it using balloons. Keep your thinking cap on. How else can you experiment using balloons?

Glossary

activity – something you do for fun or to learn about something.

congratulations – something you say to someone who has done well or accomplished something.

grab – to take hold of something suddenly.

grid – a pattern with rows of squares, such as a checkerboard.

probably – very likely to happen.

repeat – to do or say something again.

static electricity – electricity that is on an object, often created by rubbing the object against something.

stretch – to get bigger or longer.

swirl – to whirl or to move smoothly in circles.

wedge – to push or squeeze something into a small space.